MW00892378

THIS BOOK IS BELONGS TO:

Made in the USA
Monee, IL
10 May 2022

96176415R00069